a thesaurus for the way water returns
by sarah "sam" saltiel

a thesaurus for the way water returns

Copyright © 2020 by Sarah "Sam" Saltiel
All rights reserved. No part of this publication may be reproduced, distributed, or transmitted in any form or by any means, including photocopying, recording, or other electronic or mechanical methods, without the prior written permission of the publisher, except in the case of brief quotations embodied in critical reviews and certain other noncommercial uses permitted by copyright law.

First Printing, 2020
Printing information available on the last page.

ISBN 978-1-989795-03-3 (sc)
ISBN 978-1-989795-05-7 (hc)
ISBN 978-1-989795-04-0 (e)

Riza Publishing Press
Ottawa, ON, Canada
www.rizapress.com

TABLE OF CONTENTS

JULY..7
AUGUST...12
SEPTEMBER...16
OCTOBER...25
NOVEMBER..30

a thesaurus for the way water returns

JULY

the week i move to the desert, i buy strawberries and leave them in the fridge for days.

they are still   red   when i find them, seeds littering the
plastic container like
rat drop pings,
i   drop breath, step

outside and i stay dry,
                    try   to remember this is not chicago,

        i   did   not   stay,

      things don't decay
      here, things boil and brine—i
            enshrine in my own dust.

in my home, everything is mine and
        not mine.

      i cling to my morning coffee because it burns my throat down—
      skeleton bleach myself with another one when i get to work,
      possessed by the pain, i barely notice the heat,
      i am flesh stripping—almost—   tipping—

* * *

that week you call to say you broke up with your girlfriend.

    i lie on the floor of my living room as we talk because
i don't yet have chairs and

        i want to tell you that i love you,
        want to tell you that
        my carpet turns my arms red and sore
like
        spider bites,
        and that your breath feels like a wind
that doesn't exist here,

i wind your words
    against my fear, pull them tight to cut off the blood.

        at night i press ice cubes against my
            forehead,
            wrists,
        the insides of my thighs, reliving

you.
flesh dripping to relieve—   i consume you in sighs—

        i try

        to tell you

i'm sorry that i treat every word between us
like it is the difference between surviving and not.

i size you up, line my body with you like an ache—
    finally— one that i recognize.

        * * *

a thesaurus for the way water returns

my mother comes to help me unpack,
i unbody myself from the cardboard boxes and packing peanuts,
shattering

        on the ground (like leaves), disappearing myself like steam,
            i scream

                (when she leaves),
i walk down the street and look at buildings ?grounded? surrounded by the
fact that people really live here and make this their home
instead of being play actors
disappearing between the splintered columns of stage sets.
i touch the spines of a cactus because i posit
that it is paper mache and it will collapse

like my cardboard boxes,   ready to crumble
in the next summer rain.

i take to sc   atter   ing

        things   in places where they don't belong—

        (leave my backpack)   in the bathroom
        just to make sure that nobody moves my props when
        i'm gone.
when i come back home everything is as i left it but i feel
    scattered,
                unpropped—

        my cat keeps me anchored in time and space.
        i know if i died(?)
        she would be hungry and that hunger keeps me
        rooted—i hunger—rooted.   each time
                                                      i cross
                                                    the threshold,

        i have to double back twice.
        the first time to check the lock,
        the second to check the air.

sarah "sam" saltiel

    i stand in my doorway, seeing flashes of a future where i forget it one day and return to find my cat boiled alive in the place that is supposed(?) to be our home.

when   ?   the rain does come.

it pools in the windowsill near my bed, the one that i forgot to close.
i lie on my back in the thick dark,

    and fugitive rain drops melt holes in my cheeks.

* * *

a thesaurus for the way water returns

YOUFLOODME

* * *

sarah "sam" saltiel

AUGUST

                    i visit chicago, then return.

i am excised from my past here,
it is not a relief.
it's like missing a tongue with which i could say the words if only
i knew what they were(?)

i come back with a still-bleeding tattoo.
i wake up digging my fingernails into the peeling skin of my wrist so i bite down
to fight the itch— there's something that i like about inking myself into
        an open wound.

                                      * * *

a thesaurus for the way water returns

when it gets hottest, i start kickboxing for my anger.
most of what that accomplishes is that i fantasize about my kickboxing instructor pinning me on the ground because it's less complicated than fantasizing about you.

>when i wrapped my legs around your hips,
>you said: You don't know how long I've been
>wanting to do this

but also, after,

>when you held me— or didn't hold me,
>lying naked beside me, arm performing intimacy but

>barely   touching,

you told me about the moment that you first knew
that you loved your ex.

>i don't know if i will ever be more colorful to you
>than her residue on your body.

when i lie on my bed in the desert with the sun strip-splitting me,
my hand trickling between my legs...

>instead

i think about how she and i live in different cities from you now
but you don't have the space to carry both of us with you
and it is too hard to masturbate to my own heaviness.

sarah "sam" saltiel

        i want   (?)
                            you

to hold me in your hand like a rock that you picked up in the stream.
       i want to talisman you, but i erase with water.

before we fucked,
you told me about tar trickling down your brain and
i think maybe (?) when you touch me, i come away sticky too.

i hope that we didn't love each other because we were both dripping
with tar   and tar recognizes itself,
wants to join until it drowns in a wave—

i come back from chicago in a wave of knowing the thing you loved the
most about me was that i was the opposite of loneliness.

* * *

a thesaurus for the way water returns

i cry more days than not and
i sleep on the couch for nights, just

        because i can,

watching 13 reasons why because it's like poking a loose tooth
with your tongue until you feel the nerve root-   ripping
from your gums. poke it again and you taste your insides.
i lose both tooth and tongue.

i sleep in different parts of my apartment every night:
the bed,

        the couch,

                the bean bag, as if

        i can leave enough of an echo in each room
        that this place will start to feel like mine
        and not like someone else's skin that i wear on top of my own.

i would sleep on the floor if it meant that my breath and sweat would seep
into the ground enough for me to see myself in it,
i want to be stuck,

        struck into this desert but like dust, i dissipate.

                * * *

sarah "sam" saltiel

SEPTEMBER

two months of twisting my key in the lock,
i believe each time that it won't open,
that i will find
that i'm trying to gain access to someone else's home. two months,

                         and i'm still deciding which side of the
           bed is mine.

i have started kissing people who aren't you—

one of them

holds me the way i have been wanting to be held for years—holds me like (?) it matters?
not like we were two forces of energy that happened to come together and bounce off just as easily, hurtling
back into the darkness from whence we came.

i don't know?
how to lie next to his kindness but
                that kindness has chosen the right side of the bed so
      that is a start.

one of them

is the man who assaulted me when i was fifteen—
he is only one of my worst memories that i have returned to years later,
poking it and stripping it down again in the name of catharsis.
we skype on the weekends and i text him after i hang up, telling him how much i want to fuck him.

a thesaurus for the way water returns

the other day, he told me that he wants to sink inside me with his hand on my neck. i rainwater froze even though
                              ?

                              it has been years   ?

it has been years since i have had sex without a hand on my neck—
my breath is the perfect handhold to get a grasp on how much i want them/i want...
i tar trickled and tried
                to answer as if he was a different person,
                as if sexting him wasn't an act of overwriting
                                and rewriting.

two months of unsticking myself from my bed,
there is a week—i am weak—
                when i cannot bring myself to speak to anyone.

it scares me like nothing else because i don't know
anyone who has loved me
                        and not loved me for my words,
                so what am i left with when they're gone?
                what will happen to me when i am
                hanging upside down and my words are
                drained from me like gravity? what
                happens when i un   sti   ck?

                          * * *

sarah "sam" saltiel

as the last nights of september drain away, i drink half a bottle of red
wine by myself/use the other half to cook pumpkin meat because
i don't want to leave it gutted/un   used. i wake up in the
middle of the night with eyes blacked out but

> i can still smell pumpkin, red wine,
> and heavy cream,
> and it nearly make me sick/the
> food spoils and curdles, boils into
> my dreams/i wake up with breaths
> pacing miles back and forth along
> the prison of my throat — i rot
> away (decay?)

during the day, i drink chamomile tea at work
to avoid having panic attacks and
i spend one morning translating a review for our zombie game, shifting
their words through a sieve until they look like something i recognize.
the words shuffle on google translate but in the mess of misplaced adjectives
and incorrect conjugations it says:
Trauma tells the price we paid to be alive.

a thesaurus for the way water returns

i wake   again grasping for my phone, mind swept of history like the raising of the dead.

pretending that i am not stuck in a cycle of tortured nights and rites
to say in the morning
to try

                to try to find the energy—

                try— to leave my bed.

                    * * *

sarah "sam" saltiel

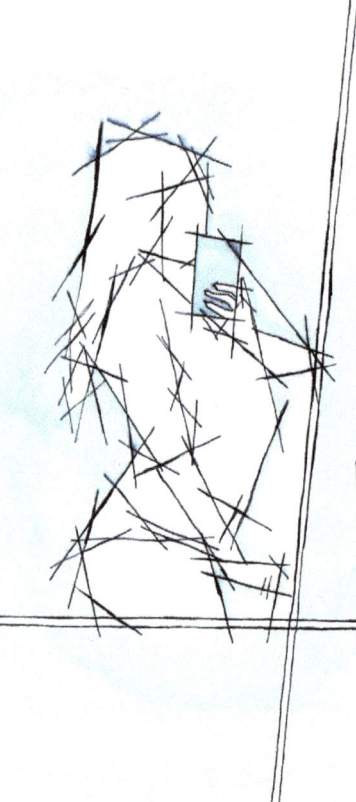

i've started taking photos of myself in the reflective surfaces of my home. over and over, as if i have something to prove.

a thesaurus for the way water returns

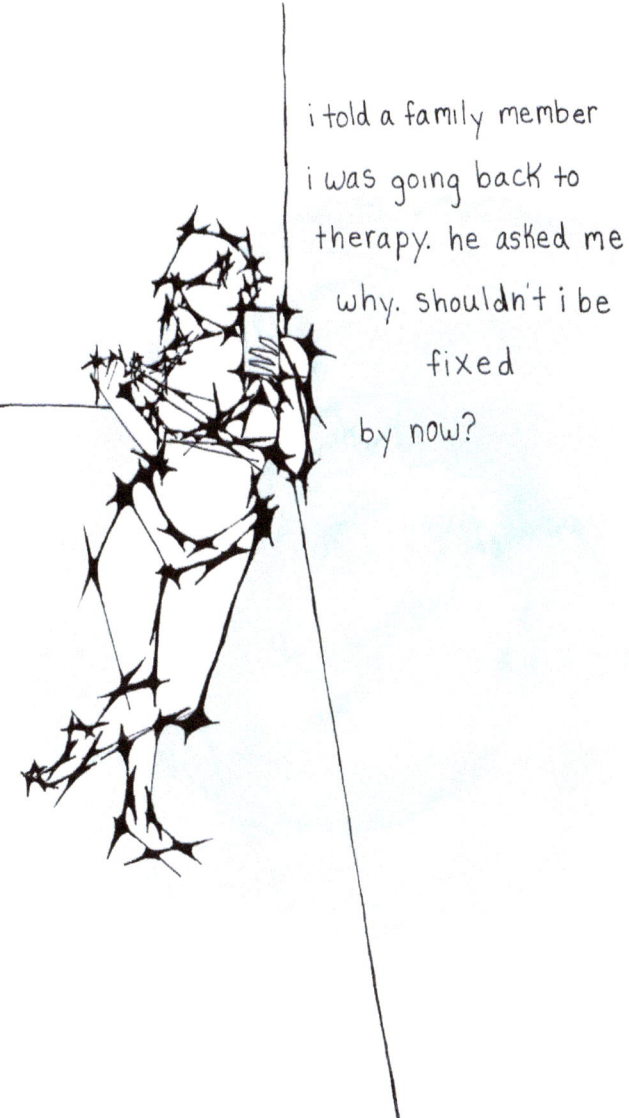

i told a family member i was going back to therapy. he asked me why. shouldn't i be fixed by now?

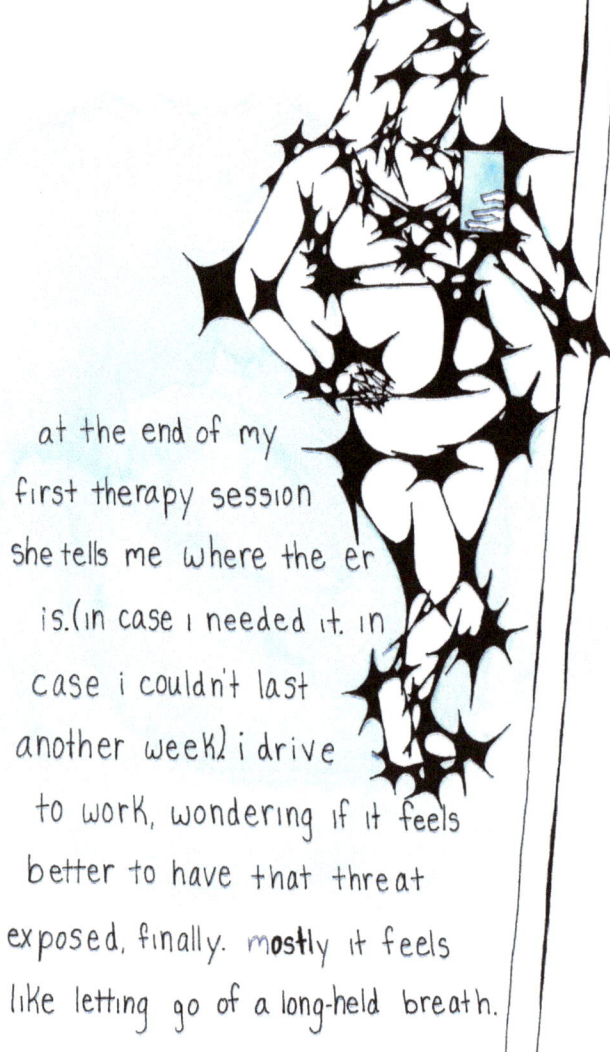

at the end of my first therapy session she tells me where the er is. (in case i needed it. in case i couldn't last another week) i drive to work, wondering if it feels better to have that threat exposed, finally. mostly it feels like letting go of a long-held breath.

a thesaurus for the way water returns

i try to cut back on my drinking because i don't like waking up in the morning, realizing i drink with the desperation of someone trying to drown.

a thesaurus for the way water returns

OCTOBER

this is the year i fall in love twice and i am left

        wondering
        how i can start to love (?)

someone in a city that only exists in my past, temporally and physically displaced, disjointed, i unmake that space, writing more words to him than he knows what to do with—

                              d   r

                                        aining—

i don't know how to love someone   except
by giving them as many of my words as possible. i have a google doc
of all the beautiful sentences i've collected and every time i think i
could love someone, i send it to them, hoping to find someone that will
understand what it means that they have my words, that they will not
take that lightly, but i—

the "you" changes. i ache.

                      * * *

sarah "sam" saltiel

i return to chicago once more.
i populate the corners of my vision
with the people i know aren't there anymore,
each stranger's face morphing into someone who left, like me, until the
campus turns into the landscape of my memory and i can reimagine it as a
place where i was happy.

at the same time, some part of me believes that just behind that apartment
door that i no longer have the key to is our fridge, with the
mouldy bloody mary mix.

                                     i live there
                                                     still,

drinking tea to ward off my thoughts, and sinking into oblivion in our
living room couch (but i drink tea in the desert now—
i sink)

i find my echoes everywhere throughout the city, stretched thin and
superimposed,
                                           i try to breathe

                       through them,
            opening my mouth to saran wrap scream—

visiting now means smelling like the shampoo of a different person
every day and having the patterns of each of my friends' couches
imprinted on my cheek,   trying to forget

                                         for a week—
               * * *

a thesaurus for the way water returns

in chicago, i wish i could better remember the things that you say to me when we're both drunk. you said something about being in love with me and maybe it was a joke and maybe it wasn't, but all i remember is that i laughed in response and said, That's not true.

i think you wait until i'm drunk to say things like that to me because you know that my memory streams away—

>when i crawled into bed next to you,
>it's as if there had never been any hesitation at all,
>as if you hadn't told me that we shouldn't sleep together.
>immediately, your hand was on my hip and moving and i
>wanted you and i told you as much.

>we were so drunk that i told you that i would teach you
>how to make me cum and then immediately forgot.
>you brought it up the next day and i just shrugged it off
>because i couldn't say, I'll show you next time,

>>because ?
>>there wasn't supposed to be a *this* time but

i want   (you)

i want to kiss you while i'm sober to remember the way you place your hands, i—

and i want to cum for you like a f   l   o   o   d—

sarah "sam" saltiel

two days after getting high with you, returned home,
i crawl under my desk at work and have a panic attack because lying next to you in the dark fitting my fingers into the dips in your bones felt a kind of profound such that i didn't know what i could possibly say to you anymore.

> what could follow smiling at each other in the dark while softly singing along to chance the rapper's sunday candy? how can i follow?

when i closed my eyes, i could see blood vessels filling up and bursting but
i
spent
centuries

> 1. counting
> 2. your ribs and
> 3. feeling them fill up with your breaths.
> 4. i had to keep moving my hand along your stomach and back again to ensure myself that you wouldn't break,
> 5. i rehomed in your body.

a thesaurus for the way water returns

as much as i hope for a someday with you, i know there is none
    ?hope?

        so i say   ?
        i am happy enough to sit on your kitchen floor
        in my socks
        and oversized sweatshirt,
eating a frozen banana because you told me that i had to eat
something, while you stand a few feet away, cooking dinner and tapping
your foot along to my music— after i leave,
        after i *after* you, i move on to the next day.

how? can i follow?

        * * *

sarah "sam" saltiel

NOVEMBER

i have taken to telling my friends that if a point comes when they want to be gone from me, that it's ok and i understand, but to tell me
because i cannot stand the pain of not knowing and i hope that they
will give me that and that i will give them the same. i tell you that too,
and i pass in and out of an apartment where boiling showers freeze my skin
in an instant and the kitchen sink only pours out water hot enough
to hurt, and then drips for hours after i turn it off, each drop aching for
pink skin, wanting to blister and bubble. i wash my dishes in the middle
of the night, and outside my door, i hear wild dogs, growling. i want to
talk to you about what happened between us but i cower. i wash my
dishes and clean my apartment and i

                am working on

                      forgiving myself the way that my cat does
        when i feed her every night at midnight because
        it might be late, but i still feed her every day,
        and every day i wake up and continue to sit with
        my own brain—

i download an app to manage my self harm and panic attacks. i open it one night, sitting with rain inside my head, hiding my body in the couch my mother gave me when she came. i word wedge myself into it, waiting, waiting for a blank screen to load.

about the poet

Sarah "Sam" Saltiel is a queer, nonbinary artist and writer based in Albuquerque, New Mexico. Graduated from the University of Chicago with degrees in English, Visual Arts, and Creative Writing, Saltiel grapples with with questions of gender and mental illness, particularly pertaining to what it means to be a body in space. She seeks to investigate matters of identity, intersection, and erasure through a wide variety of mediums.

Saltiel has been publishing since 2013 and has works published with Duende, Thoreau's Rooster, and Storm of Blue Press, among others. All of her work can be found on her professional facebook page, or on her website: sarahsamsaltiel.com

praise for *a thesaurus for the way water returns*

"This book moved me. It was deeply personal and achingly beautiful, and by the time it was over I was wishing for more. "i don't know how to love someone except by giving them as many of my words as possible." Thank you for giving us your words, Sarah. They inspired me."
    - Hinnah Mian, author of *To Build a Home*

"This short collection is one with unforgettable promise. With the elements and tone of intimate diary entries, the writing exhibited here is an honest, realistic telling of someone's personal journey through the torments of love, acceptance and the art of moving on. I couldn't recommend it more. If you are looking for a beautifully candid read look no further."
    - Shannon Ellis, author of *Elements of an Adored Mind*

"Saltiel pulls deep to bring you a collection of events as real as they are relatable. Every page reads like a confessional. This is not just a book of poetry- it is an open view into the heart of somebody hurting and, more importantly, healing. It is honest, point-blank, and raw; the perfect combination."
    - Beth Huston, founder of *Pen and Pendulum*

www.ingramcontent.com/pod-product-compliance
Lightning Source LLC
Chambersburg PA
CBHW061212070526
44583CB00025B/3225